Published 2002 by Grolier Educational
Sherman Turnpike,
Danbury, Connecticut 06816

© 2002 Brown Partworks Limited

FOR BROWN PARTWORKS

Project editor:	Lisa Magloff
Deputy editor:	Jane Scarsbrook
Text editors:	Caroline Beattie, Ben Morgan,
Designer:	Joan Curtis
Picture researcher:	Liz Clachan
Illustrations:	Mark Walker
Index:	Kay Ollerenshaw
Design manager:	Lynne Ross
Production manager:	Matt Weyland
Managing editor:	Bridget Giles
Editorial director:	Anne O'Daly
Consultant:	Donald R. Franceschetti, PhD University of Memphis

Printed and bound in Hong Kong

Set ISBN 0-7172-5608-1
Volume ISBN 0-7172-5611-1

Library of Congress Cataloging-in-Publication Data
Science Activities / Grolier Educational
   p. cm.
   Includes index.
   Contents: v.1. Electricity and magnetism—v.2. Everyday Chemistry—v.3. Force and motion—v.4. Heat and energy—v.5. Inside matter—v.6. Light and color—v.7. Our Environment—v.8. Sound and hearing—v.9. Using materials—v.10. Weather and climate.
ISBN 0-7172-5608-1 (set : alk.paper)—ISBN 0-7172-5609-X (v.1 : alk. paper)—
ISBN 0-7172-5610-3 (v.2 : alk. paper)—ISBN 0-7172-5611-1 (v.3 : alk. paper)—ISBN
0-7172-5612-X (v.4 : alk. paper)—ISBN 0-7172-5613-8 (v.5 : alk. paper)—ISBN
0-7172-5614- 6 (v.6 : alk. paper)—ISBN 0-7172-5615-4 (v.7 : alk. paper)—ISBN
0-7172-5616-2 (v.8 : alk. paper)—ISBN 0-7172-5617-0 (v.9 : alk. paper)—ISBN
0-7172-5618-9 (v.10 : alk. paper)
   1. Science—Study and teaching—Activity programs—Juvenile literature. [1. Science—Experiments. 2. Experiments] I. Grolier Educational (Firm)

LB1585.S335 2002
507.1'2—dc21

2001040519

ABOUT THIS SET

Science Activities gives children a chance to explore fascinating topics from the world of science using the same methods that professional scientists use to solve problems. This set introduces young scientists to the scientific method by focusing on the importance of planning experiments, conducting them in a rigorous fashion so that a fair test can be carried out, recording all the stages, and organizing and analyzing the data to draw conclusions. Readers will have the chance to conduct exciting and innovative hands-on activities and to learn how to record and analyze their experiments and results in a variety of ways.

Every volume of *Science Activities* contains 10 step-by-step experiments, along with follow-up activities that encourage readers to find out more about the subject. The activities are explained and enhanced with detailed introductory and analysis sections. Colorful photos illustrate each activity, and every book is packed full of pictures and illustrations explaining the details of each topic.

By working fun and educational experiments into the context of the scientific method, anyone using this set can get a feel for how professional scientists go about their work. Most importantly, just have fun!

PICTURE CREDITS
(b=bottom; t=top)

AKG London: British Library 5; **Art Explosion:** 56; **Corbis:** 43, Betteman Archive 27, Gerald French 51, Todd Gipstein 12, George Hall 11, Charles Lenars 29, Barry Lewis 44, Buddy Mays 38, Kevin R. Morris 4, Steven E. Sutton front cover, 13, Michael S. Yamashita 49, 55; **Ecoscene:** Anthony Cooper 21; **Image Bank:** Jeff Cadge 28, Colour Day 50, Clint Eley 17, Herbert Hartman 39, Jeff Hunter 6, Joseph Van Os 16, Jose Szkodzinski 57; **Janine Weidel Photo Library:** 21; **Leslie Garland Picture Library:** 22; **NOAA:** 61; **Science Photo Library:** Colin Cuthbert 20; **Sylvia Cordaiy:** Johnathan Smith 7; **Travel Ink:** Derek Alan 33.

CONTENTS

VOLUME 3
FORCE AND MOTION

INTRODUCTION

Forces start objects moving, change the way they move, and bring them to a halt. Even when you stand still, you are pushed and pulled by forces. In these pages we will find out just how forces work.

The world around us is always in motion. Some of this movement can be observed—cars drive by, clouds move in the sky, and water flows in rivers. Other movement is not so noticeable. When you are sitting in a quiet room, everything seems still, but the particles inside the atoms that make up the room and your body are constantly on the move. The room itself is on a planet that spins on its axis and orbits the Sun, while the universe is expanding all the time. Scientists call the study of all these types of movement dynamics.

The causes of changes in the speed or direction of movement are called forces. Machines have been used for thousands of years to magnify or change the direction of a force to help people do certain tasks. Ramps, levers, bridges, and pulleys are examples of simple machines. You can find out how they work in activities 6 through 9 (pages 33 through 55).

FIRST FINDINGS

Only in the past 500 years have people fully understood how these machines work. In ancient Greece the philosopher Aristotle thought that an object only

The picture above uses a long exposure to show traffic speeding along in Taipei, Taiwan. As we find new ways to harness forces, the pace of life has increased.

moved when it was pushed or pulled by a force. He thought that as soon as the force was taken away, the object would stop moving. However, this did not explain events in the real world.

It wasn't until the 17th century that Italian scientist Galileo Galilei was able to explain this movement. He realized that when an object slows down or speeds up, it is the result of a number of forces acting on it: A stone is made to move by the force of a thrower's arm. As it moves, the force of gravity pulls the stone toward the center of Earth. The stone is also slowed by air resistance.

Galileo realized that without these forces slowing moving objects down and pulling them toward the ground, they would keep moving in a straight line. He came up with the theory that objects change their speed only when a force acts on them. He also proposed the idea that an object keeps accelerating (speeding up) or decelerating (slowing down) as long as the forces acting on it do not cancel each other out.

Building on Galileo's ideas, English scientist Isaac Newton came up with three laws to explain how everything moves. They were published in his book *The Mathematical Principles of Natural Philosophy* (usually shortened to *The Principia*). Newton's first two laws followed Galileo's ideas. Newton's third law states that when a force is applied to an object, an equal force is exerted in the opposite direction. You can find out more about Newton's laws when you build the jet boat in activity 1 (pages 6 through 11) and explore why some objects float in activity 10 (pages 56 through 61).

Isaac Newton published The Principia in 1687. Volume One included his three laws of motion.

Newton also explained in greater detail how the force of gravity pulls objects toward large bodies such as the Earth. You can explore some of the more unusual effects of gravity when you build the pendulums in activities 4 and 5 (pages 22 though 32).

CHALLENGING NEWTON

As scientists began to delve inside the atom and explore how objects move in space, they discovered problems with Newton's laws. At the start of the 20th century the German scientist Albert Einstein explained how light moves in his two theories of relativity. His findings showed that Newton's laws could not be applied to all types of movement. Einstein's theories work very well in explaining the motion of planets, stars, galaxies, and the universe.

Other scientists, such as the German Max Planck, developed quantum theory to explain how the tiny particles inside the atom move. One of the greatest scientific challenges of today is to come up with one theory that will connect all these forces. Called the Grand Unified Theory (GUT), it has yet to be figured out by anyone.

The good science guide

Science is not only a collection of facts—it is the process that scientists use to gather information. Follow this good science guide to get the most out of each experiment.

• Carry out each experiment more than once. This prevents accidental mistakes skewing the results. The more times you carry out an experiment, the easier it will be to see if your results are accurate.

• Decide how you will write down your results. You can use a variety of different methods, such as descriptions, diagrams, tables, charts, and graphs. Choose the methods that will make your results easy to read and understand.

• Be sure to write your results down as you are doing the experiment. If one of the results seems very different from the others, it could be because of a problem with the experiment that you should fix immediately.

• Drawing a graph of your results can be very useful because it helps fill in the gaps in your experiment. Imagine, for example, that you plot time along the bottom of the graph and temperature up the side. If you measure the temperature ten times, you can put the results on the graph as dots. Use a ruler to draw a straight line through all the dots. You can now estimate what happened in between each dot, or measurement, by picking any point along the line and reading the time and temperature for that point from the sides of the graph.

• Learn from your mistakes. Some of the most exciting findings in science came from an unexpected result. If your results do not tally with your predictions, try to find out why.

• You should always be careful when carrying out or preparing any experiment, whether it is dangerous or not. Make sure you know the safety rules before you start working.

• Never begin an experiment until you have talked to an adult about what you are going to do.

ACTIVITY 1
ON THE MOVE

When a space shuttle lifts off, its engines create a force so colossal that the whole shuttle is pushed into space. The way forces affect how an object moves depends on three simple laws.

Newton's laws of motion explain how all everyday objects move. Today we know that the three laws of motion do not always apply—tiny particles smaller than atoms, for instance, seem to obey very different laws. However, Newton's laws do explain most types of movement that you can see and feel. The three laws are the basic science that was used to send craft into space; without them astronauts may never have reached the Moon.

A space shuttle lifts off from Kennedy Space Center in Florida, propelled by the blast of burning gas from its fuel tanks.

Newton's first law says that if an object is not pushed or pulled by a force, it will either stay still or keep moving in a straight line at a constant speed. For example, a space shuttle on a launch pad will sit still until its engine fires and forces it upward. This tendency of objects to stay still or keep going is called inertia. In space inertia can make a spacecraft carry on moving forever at the same speed unless the craft uses its engine to slow down or speed up, or it bumps into something. Motion on Earth is a bit more complicated—objects have to move through air or water, which slows them. At the same time, gravity pulls them downward.

Newton's second law explains how an object either speeds up or slows down when a force acts on it. The change of speed depends on the size of the force and the object's mass. Mass is the amount of matter an object contains. A car is more massive than a bicycle, so a bigger force is needed to make it speed up or slow down.

The third law says that every action has an equal, opposite reaction. This is how the space shuttle works. The blast of burning gas from its engine is the action. The shuttle's movement is the reaction.

You can study Newton's laws of motion in the following activity by building your own jet boat.

Speedboats get their power from a rotating blade called a propeller. The propeller pushes water backward, causing a reaction force that pushes the boat forward.

What a drag!

On Earth moving objects must battle against air and water resistance, which slows them down. This force is called drag. Many boats, airplanes, trains, and automobiles are designed with a smooth shape that reduces drag as much as possible.

The diagram below shows a moving car. As it travels, it pushes against the air, causing drag. The drag means the car must use more force and energy to maintain its speed. One way of reducing drag is to shape the car so that air flows smoothly over it. This is called streamlining—it allows air to flow freely, like a stream, with the minimum of resistance.

Many animals have streamlined bodies to reduce drag, especially animals that fly, swim, or run very fast. Water causes much more drag than air, so aquatic animals are the most streamlined of all. To cope with their environment, most fish have torpedo-shaped bodies that enable them to slip through water with the minimum effort. Their scales are also coated in slime, which lubricates them and reduces drag even further.

Most cars have a smooth shape so that air flows easily around them and does not resist their movement too much.

Jet Boat

Goals

1. **Demonstrate Newton's laws of motion.**
2. **Find out how drag and gravity affect motion.**
3. **Build your own jet-powered boat.**

What you will need:

- *3-inch (7.5cm) plastic tube or straw that can bend without breaking*
- *rubber stopper with a hole. If you can't find one, ask an adult to make a hole in a cork.*
- *small, flat piece of styrofoam*
- *balloons of different sizes*
- *a bath, pond, or wading pool for your jet boat to zoom across!*

1 Push the tube into the rubber stopper until it nearly reaches the other side.

2 Push the free end of the tube through one end of the styrofoam tray. The tray will form the body of your boat.

Whoosh!

Most boats do not use a jet engine to power them. They use propellers that whizz around, pulling water from under the boat and pushing it to the rear. However, a few high-speed boats use a jet engine like yours. The fastest travel at 320 miles per hour (515 km per hour).

Safety tip

If you do not have a rubber stopper with a hole, you can use a cork. Cutting a hole in a cork can be tricky, so ask an adult to do it for you. He or she will find it easier to cut the cork in half first to make it shorter.

3 Inflate a small balloon, and pinch its neck or put a paper clip over the neck to keep the air inside. Don't knot the end.

Troubleshooting

My boat keeps going to one side. What can I do to make it travel in a straight line?

You can control the boat's direction by adjusting the tube slightly from side to side. For example, if the boat moves to the left, angle the tube to the right, and vice versa. If you have trouble bending the tube, leave it straight but push it through the styrofoam at an angle so that it points backward.

4 Carefully stretch the mouth of the inflated balloon over the rubber stopper. This is tricky, so you might have to keep trying. When the balloon is on, pinch the tube to keep air from leaking out.

5 Bend the tube so it points backward. Then put the boat in water and allow air to escape from the tube. If you have a large pool, you can use a long ruler or a tape measure to figure out how far the boat travels. Make a note of this distance.

FOLLOW-UP Jet boat

You can take two different measurements depending on the size of the pool or bath you are using. If you have a small pool or bath, measure the time it takes for the boat to reach the other end. If you have enough room, though, measure how far the boat gets before it stops.

There are lots of ways that you can vary this experiment and compare the results. Here are a few suggestions.

Try using different-sized balloons and drawing a graph of balloon size against the distance covered. You can measure the width of each balloon before you blow it up.

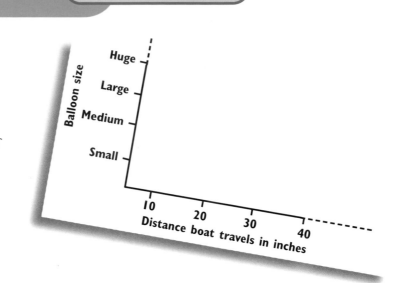

A good way to measure a balloon's size is to count how many breaths it takes to fill. Take a rest between each balloon though!

If the balloons are different shapes, measure their size by counting how many breaths you use to inflate them.

Try increasing the boat's weight by placing coins on it, then see how far it travels. (Remember the second law of motion: heavier objects need a bigger force to get them moving.)

Repeat the experiment with the end of the tube in the air instead of under water. You can do this by bending the tube upward and taping it to the back of the

You could plot a graph like this to find out if balloon size affects how far the boat travels.

boat. Does the boat travel as far when the tube is pointing into the air?

To study the effect of drag, tape squares of cardboard onto the deck of the boat. Position the squares so they are upright and facing forward to create as much air resistance as possible. What effect does this have on the distance the boat travels?

Try fastening similar squares underneath the boat so that they cause drag in the water. Does this make the boat go even slower?

If you want to try making the boat go *really* far, attach two balloons at once to it, or use one gigantic balloon.

ANALYSIS
On the move

During this activity you saw how air is forced from the balloon at the rear of the boat and pushes the boat forward. This is an example of Newton's third law, which says that every action has an equal and opposite reaction. The air shooting out of the balloon is the action; the movement of the boat in the opposite direction is the reaction. The larger the balloon, the greater the forces at work, and the farther the boat moves.

WHY DOES THE BOAT SLOW DOWN?

You will find that the boat keeps moving even after all the air has left the balloon. This is due to the boat's inertia, which is an example of Newton's first law. The boat keeps moving in the same direction unless an external force slows it down. In fact, there is an external force: drag. Eventually, drag caused by the water and the air brings the boat to a halt. The change in speed caused by drag is an example of Newton's second law at work.

MAKING SLOW BOATS

Every object has inertia—a tendency to resist changes in its motion. The more weight an object has, the more inertia it has, and the more force is needed to get it moving. When you added coins to the boat, you increased the weight and inertia, and the boat became harder to start and stop.

You should also have found that the boat traveled farther when the tube pointed into the water. Water is much thicker than air, so it took longer for all the air to leave the balloon under water, and the air kept on pushing the boat for longer, taking it farther.

Adding paper squares to the boat slowed it down by increasing its drag. If you put paper squares on the bottom of the boat, the drag would have been even greater, and the boat would have been very slow.

Parachutes slow down very fast-moving objects by creating a lot of drag.

ACTIVITY 2
ENERGY AND MOTION

Energy makes things happen. It is the ability to exert a force over a distance. There are many different forms of energy, including heat, light, electricity, and chemical energy. In this activity we look at the energy in moving objects.

Every time you travel in a car or ride a bicycle, you are using energy to make you move. A car gets its energy from gasoline, while a bicycle gets energy from the rider's body. Scientists have a special term for the energy in a moving object: kinetic energy. The faster or heavier a moving object is, the more kinetic energy it has. A jumbo jet has far more kinetic energy than a bee, for instance, because it is much heavier and faster.

Objects do not have to be moving to contain energy. Imagine pushing a bicycle up a hill. When you reach the top, you can ride down without having to pedal. You have given the bicycle a type of energy called potential energy, which means it has the po-

🔵 *In a soapbox derby the driver uses energy from the pull of gravity to make the car move forward down a slope. The moving car has kinetic energy.*

tential to move when you let it go. Clockwork toys also contain potential energy. When you wind up the spring on a clockwork toy, you store energy inside the toy. If you let go of the spring, the energy is released as kinetic energy, and the toy moves.

Energy is impossible to destroy. When you use energy, it doesn't disappear, it just changes from one kind into another. Think of cycling downhill, for instance. As your potential energy is used up, it turns into kinetic energy, making you go faster and faster. To stop the bicycle, you need to get rid of the kinetic energy. Your brakes do this by creating friction: they rub against the wheels and turn the bicycle's kinetic energy into heat energy and sound energy. Cars and trains also use friction to stop. Because they are much heavier than bicycles, they need a lot more friction, so their brakes are much noisier—especially if they stop very suddenly.

IN A SPIN

If you've ever watched an ice skater spin around, you might have noticed something odd. As the skater pulls her arms closer to her body, she spins faster, but without using any extra energy.

How is this possible if she is not gaining any extra kinetic energy? The secret lies in the way her weight is distributed. When the skater's arms are stretched out, some of her weight is moving in a very wide circle. Although her body in the middle is turning relatively slowly, her hands are moving very fast. As she draws her arms in, her hands move through a smaller circle. Since she is on a very smooth surface, there is almost no change in her kinetic energy. She revolves much faster since every part of her body is now moving in a small circle.

You can study this effect by carrying out the activity on the next page.

An ice skater spins in a wide circle, with her arms outstretched. The closer she brings her arms to her body, the faster she spins around.

The ring's tendency to fall downward and to the left spins the rollers.

The rollers are held in place but are free to turn.

Perpetual motion

For centuries people have dreamed of building a machine that would keep going forever without power—a perpetual motion machine. For example, the falling ring (right) is designed so that if you gave it an initial spin, it would keep on spinning forever. The large ring is pulled downward by gravity; but because its movement is blocked by the two rollers, they whirl around instead. The rollers should then keep the ring spinning. Like all perpetual motion machines, it doesn't work! The rings would have to move without losing kinetic energy, and that is impossible. Friction between the moving parts turns some of the energy into heat.

On a Roll!

Goals

1. **Change potential energy into kinetic energy.**
2. **Find out how the distribution of weight affects the movement of a spinning object.**

What you will need:

- two identical cylinders, such as storage tubes or metal cans, with resealable lids
- circular metal weights, such as coins or metal washers
- tape
- wooden board about 3 feet (1m) long

1 Tape six weights to the curved inner surface of the first cylinder (not inside the lid or on the bottom). Put three under the rim at one end and the other three under the opposite rim.

2 Tape a stack of 3 weights in the bottom of the second cylinder, right in the middle. It might help to tape the weights together first. Then tape another stack of 3 weights in the middle of the underside of the lid. Put the lids back on both cylinders.

3 Use books or bricks to prop up one end of the wooden board to about 1 foot (30cm) high.

4 Try rolling the cylinders down the ramp. Figure out the best place to release them so they don't roll off the edge or bump into each other.

5 Now use a watch to time the cylinders as they roll down the ramp. Make sure they start from the same place, and don't push them— just let go of them.

Troubleshooting

The cylinders run down the ramp too quickly to time. How can I slow them down?

Make the angle of the ramp shallower. The cylinders do not have to roll at top speed—you are only interested in how they gain speed in relation to each other. A shallower ramp will ensure that they roll more slowly and will give you more time to study the movement of each cylinder.

FOLLOW-UP

On a roll!

After you have sent the cylinders down the ramp at the same time to see which one arrives at the bottom first, send them down the ramp one at a time. Use a stopwatch to time them, and write the results in a table (see right). Repeat the experiment with the ramp at a different height.

Try placing the weights in different positions. You could put all the weights in a row from the top to the bottom of a cylinder, put them all at one end, or space them out on the lid and bottom. Before you roll each cylinder down the ramp, look at the results you already have, and try to predict what will happen. Then roll the cylinders and see if you were right. You could also try the experiment with different amounts of weight in each cylinder.

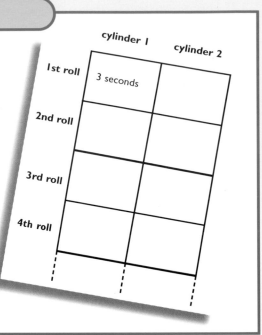

	cylinder 1	cylinder 2
1st roll	3 seconds	
2nd roll		
3rd roll		
4th roll		

ANALYSIS

Energy and motion

At the start of the experiment the two cylinders had the same potential energy because they weighed the same and started at the same height. But they didn't pick up speed in the same way. That is because of the way the weight was arranged in each cylinder.

The cylinder with coins in the center of the lid and bottom rolled faster. Its weight was in the middle, so the coins were traveling in a straight line. In contrast, the coins in the other cylinder turned through wide circles as the cylinder rolled, so they had farther to travel. The two cylinders had the same kinetic energy, and the coins themselves traveled at about the same speed, but the coins' different locations affected how fast the cylinders could roll.

You can also use a swivel chair to demonstrate what is happening in this activity. Sit in the chair, and get someone to push it around. Start with your arms stretched out as you spin, then slowly pull in your arms. Can you guess what will happen before you try it?

Potential energy

The rock in this picture has potential energy. Although it is not moving, it is sitting at the top of a slope and would roll downhill if someone pushed it hard enough. This type of potential energy is due to the force of gravity, but there are other ways of storing potential energy. Windup toys, batteries, and stretched rubber bands all have potential energy.

ACTIVITY 3
GYROSCOPE

The world is full of objects that rotate, like wheels, spinning tops, and propellers. Even Earth itself is rotating. In this activity you make a gyroscope to study how forces affect spinning objects.

Moving objects have a tendency to keep moving in the same direction at the same speed. This is called linear momentum. Imagine you are pushing a shopping cart. Once the cart gets moving, it is easy to push; but to make it turn, you have to stop it and then push it in a new direction. The cart has a tendency to keep moving in a straight line—it has linear momentum.

Now imagine you have filled the cart with heavy groceries. Because it weighs more, the cart has greater linear momentum, and it is even harder to stop it or turn it around.

If you shove the handle of a shopping cart to one side, the cart will spin around instead of moving forward. The tendency of a spinning object such as this to continue spinning is called angular momentum. A spinning object will keep spinning at a constant rate unless forces, such as friction, act to slow it down.

A spinning top stays upright because of angular momentum. The top's momentum holds it in the same position so strongly the top resists the force of gravity. Once the top starts to lose momentum, it

🔵 *A spinning top can stand upright on a very narrow base because its rotating motion gives it angular momentum.*

wobbles and falls over. The force that normally stops a spinning top is friction, caused by the base rubbing against the ground as the spinning top turns.

A gyroscope is a complex spinning top. It consists of a spinning wheel inside a set of metal rings called a gimbal (see page 20) that lets the wheel tilt freely in any direction. Like a spinning top, a gyroscope has angular momentum, so it will resist any attempt to change its direction of spin. You can place a spinning gyroscope on the tip of your finger, and it will balance perfectly, kept upright by angular momentum. If you try to push a gyroscope over, it will turn at right angles from the direction you push it, since its angular momentum tries to keep it steady. This sideways movement is called precession. The gimbal of a gyroscope may turn in slow circles because of precession due to the force of gravity.

In the following activity you turn yourself into a human gyroscope. A bicycle wheel will serve as the spinning part of the gyroscope, and your body will become a gimbal when you sit on a swivel chair.

A Human Gyroscope

Goals

1. **Find out how angular momentum affects spinning objects.**
2. **Feel the force of precession.**
3. **Turn yourself into a human gyroscope.**

What you will need:

- *bicycle wheel*
- *rubber stoppers or corks*
- *swivel chair that moves easily*
- *an assistant*

1 Hold a bicycle wheel by the axles (the metal rods that join the wheel to the bicycle). If they are too small, use corks or rubber stoppers to make small handles.

2 Sit on the swivel chair with your feet on the ground, and get a friend to spin the wheel. Be very careful not to get your fingers caught in the spokes.

Spinning satellites

Some satellites are put into a deliberate spin to keep them stable. Acting like large gyroscopes, they are less likely to drift off course as they orbit Earth. The satellites that beam phone calls around the world have to stay over the exact same place all the time. They contain spinning disks called momentum wheels that fine-tune the satellite's position. Speeding up or slowing down the momentum wheel makes the satellite turn very slightly.

Safety tip

BEWARE! This experiment can be dangerous. When the wheel is spinning quickly, it will be difficult to stop. Don't try to stop it by gripping the tire with your hand. Although this is a good example of friction causing heat energy, it will burn your skin! Never put your fingers in the spokes or even near them. To stop the wheel, let it rub on the ground—you'll see how much friction it can cause.

Autopilot

Gyroscopes help pilots fly long distances. Every airliner is equipped with an autopilot that keeps it flying straight and level along the course selected by the pilots. At the heart of the autopilot is a very fast-spinning gyroscope that always points in the same direction. If the plane goes off course, the gyroscope detects this movement, and the autopilot can then bring the plane back on course without the pilot having to do anything.

3 With the wheel held upright, lift your feet. Then tilt the wheel, and watch what happens to the chair.

Troubleshooting

I tried the experiment with the wheel, but the chair didn't move. What is going wrong?

Your chair is probably too stiff to turn easily. You could put oil on the chair's bearings (with permission) or try another chair. Or ask someone to give the chair a push to get you going at the start. Spinning the wheel more quickly would help and so would a bigger wheel. But be careful—make sure you can hold the wheel comfortably.

FOLLOW-UP A human gyroscope

There are many experiments you can try with the wheel and chair. Try tilting the wheel in different directions and at different angles. Write down what happens each time, and note what direction the chair moves. It might be easier to record your results on drawings.

Try spinning the wheel in the opposite direction. Does the chair move in the opposite direction, too?

Try spinning the chair first, and then see what effect the wheel has on its speed. With practice you might be able to speed up or slow the chair by the way you tilt the wheel.

To explore circular motion further, buy a toy gyroscope from your local toy store or a science museum.

The main difference between your bicycle wheel and a real gyroscope (apart from size) is the gimbal that surrounds the spinning center. The gimbal makes a spinning gyroscope easy to handle and helps you carry out experiments that would be impossible with a bicycle wheel.

Tie one end of your gyroscope to a piece of string, then hang the string from a secure object, like the edge of a table. Make sure the gyroscope isn't touching the ground. Get the gyroscope spinning, then let go and watch what happens. As if by magic, the gyroscope will

gimbal

rise up and spin at right angles to the string, appearing to defy gravity. Watch carefully and you'll notice something else. The gyroscope will move slowly around the string. This is precession, caused by the force of gravity. Hold the gyroscope so that it can't precess, and you'll feel the force pulling against you.

ANALYSIS
Gyroscope

In this activity you studied how a gyroscope moves. The chair and your body were the gimbal for the gyroscope.

When you lifted your feet from the floor and tilted the bicycle wheel, you should have found that the chair started to turn around. This movement is precession. Just as a gyroscope turns sideways when you try to change its direction of spin, the chair began turning when you changed the bicycle wheel's direction of spin. If you tried spinning the wheel in the

opposite direction, you would have found that the chair turned the opposite way too.

You can feel the force of precession by standing on the ground and tilting the bicycle wheel. First try this when the wheel isn't spinning. Then spin the wheel and try again. The spinning wheel's powerful angular momentum will make it surprisingly difficult to tilt. The force you feel pulling at your arms as you try to tilt the wheel is the same force that caused precession when you were in the chair.

▶ *This fairground ride is a giant gyroscope. The gimbal stays in one spot, but the person inside spins around.*

All rotating objects are influenced by the same forces that affect gyroscopes. Earth's angular momentum, for example, keeps our planet pointing in the same direction all the time as it spins. Earth spins around an imaginary line between the North and South Pole, called the axis. Over the course of a year, Earth's position in the Solar System changes as it orbits the Sun, but Earth's axis always points toward the same star, called the Pole Star. However, gravity from the Moon and Sun makes Earth precess very slowly. Over thousands of years Earth's axis moves in a circle away from the Pole Star and back again. That's why ancient people saw the stars in a slightly different position.

The tendency of a spinning object to resist attempts to change its direction of spin is an example of the first law of motion, which you might remember from activity one. The first law of motion says that an object will stay at rest or keep moving in a straight line unless a force acts on it. The same law also works for spinning objects—they keep spinning around until a force stops them turning. All the planets in the Solar System are moving this way. Because there is almost no friction in space to slow them down, they will carry on spinning for trillions of years.

Wobbly ride

Bicycles rely on angular momentum to stay upright. It is very difficult to balance on a bicycle when it is not moving—try it and see. But as soon as the bicycle starts to move, its wheels act like gyroscopes and keep it stable. The faster you travel, and the bigger and heavier the bicycle wheels, the more stable the bicycle. This is why the first bikes had huge wheels.

Modern racing bicycles have thin wheels and light frames. It only takes a small amount of energy to get the wheel to spin rapidly, so that more of the rider's muscle power can be used to get the bike moving forward.

Bicycle wheels also have ball-bearings in their axles to cut down friction between the wheel as it spins and the rest of the bicycle. That allows the wheel to spin more freely, so the wheel maintains greater momentum as it is propelled forward by its rider.

This unicyclist (right) has a tiny wheel and can only stay upright by balancing and by keeping the wheel moving at all times, if only for short distances.

ACTIVITY 4
PENDULUMS

Ever wondered how grandfather clocks keep accurate time? The secret is a device called a pendulum, which swings back and forth at a constant rate. The swing of a pendulum is a type of movement called vibration.

Try putting a ruler over the edge of a table and flicking the part that hangs over. The end of the ruler will flick back and forth and make a silly sound. This is an example of vibration.

Vibration simply means back-and-forth motion. Lots of objects vibrate, and each does so at its own particular rate, or frequency. If you ring a metal bell, the metal will vibrate at its natural frequency and produce a sound. No matter how hard you ring the bell, it always vibrates at the same frequency and always makes the same note.

A pendulum is an example of a vibrating object. The first person to understand how pendulums work was a scientist called Galileo, who lived in

You can see large, decorative pendulums inside some of these clocks. A pendulum is just a weight that is free to swing back and forth.

Italy 400 years ago. Galileo once noticed a chandelier swinging from the roof of a cathedral. By using his pulse as a stopwatch, he figured out that the chandelier always took the same time to complete one swing, no matter how far it moved—he had discovered its natural frequency. Galileo went on to discover that the time of a pendulum's swing depends on its length—the longer the pendulum, the slower the swing. The size of the weight and how hard the weight is pushed make no difference.

You can test Galileo's discovery for yourself with a simple pendulum made from a stone tied to string. Hang the string from the side of a table, pull the stone back a bit, then let go and time how long it takes to swing 10 times. Repeat the experiment, but pull the stone farther or use a heavier stone. The pendulum will be no quicker or slower. However, if you make the string shorter or longer, your pendulum will swing with a different frequency.

Better yet, make a human pendulum. Sit in a playground swing, keep your legs perfectly still, and ask a friend to push you. If you time yourself, you'll discover that it takes just as long to swing back and forth no matter how big the swings are.

The time that a pendulum takes to swing once is called its period, and the distance between the pendulum's resting point and the farthest point of its swing is called the amplitude. If you leave a pendulum swinging for a long time, you'll notice that its amplitude gets smaller and smaller until the pendulum comes to a stop. That is because the pendulum loses energy as a result of drag in the air and friction between the string and the point from which the pendulum hangs. However, the frequency does not change as the pendulum loses energy—the amplitude gets smaller, but the period stays the same.

TWO-PART PENDULUM

In the following activity you make a pendulum out of two connected parts. Each part acts like a separate pendulum, with its own period and amplitude, so the whole device moves in a more complicated way than a single pendulum. Instead of swinging back and forth, the two-part pendulum moves in a way that looks random. It is only when you look at the pattern its movement makes that the two-part pendulum will begin to make sense.

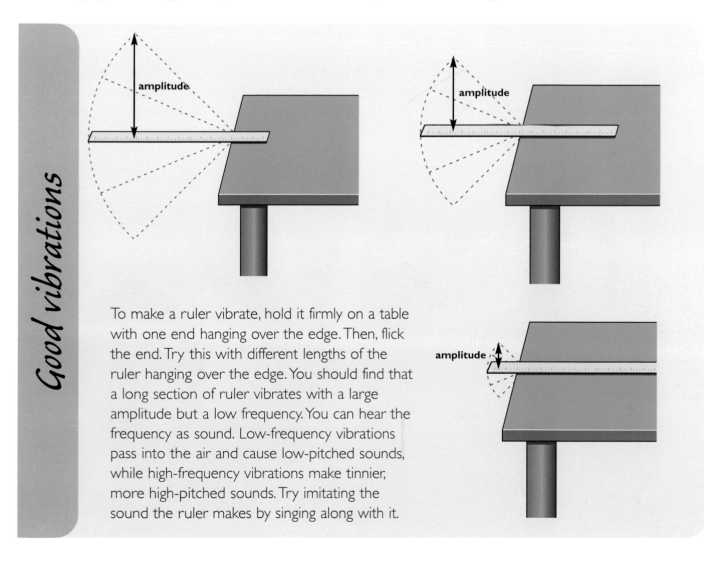

Good vibrations

To make a ruler vibrate, hold it firmly on a table with one end hanging over the edge. Then, flick the end. Try this with different lengths of the ruler hanging over the edge. You should find that a long section of ruler vibrates with a large amplitude but a low frequency. You can hear the frequency as sound. Low-frequency vibrations pass into the air and cause low-pitched sounds, while high-frequency vibrations make tinnier, more high-pitched sounds. Try imitating the sound the ruler makes by singing along with it.

Pendulum Painter

Goals

1. **Find out how pendulums move.**
2. **Build a compound pendulum.**
3. **Create amazing paint patterns.**

What you will need:

- *large paper or plastic cup*
- *hole punch*
- *string*
- *pin*
- *masking tape*
- *water-based paint*
- *large sheet of paper*
- *newspaper*

1 Make three holes around the rim of the cup with a hole punch, and tie a 3-inch (7.6cm) length of string through each hole. Knot these strings together above the cup, then tie them to the end of a 1-foot (30cm) length of string.

3 Tie a long piece of string between two walls so that it runs above a table. The string should be a bit loose in the middle. Tie the end of the cup's string to the long string so that the cup hangs over the middle of the table.

2 Make a small hole in the bottom of the plastic cup with a pin. Cover the hole with a piece of tape.

4 Cover the table with newspaper. Then place a large piece of plain paper directly under the cup. Half fill the cup with paint.

5 Pull the cup to one side, peel off the tape, then release the cup, and let it swing. The paint will dribble out and make a pattern on the paper.

6 Allow the cup to swing for one minute and then stop it and quickly cover the hole.

Troubleshooting

What if I can't hang the cup over a table?

Work on the floor. Position two chairs 2 feet (60cm) apart and back to back. Put heavy books on the seats. Tie the pendulum to the chair tops.

If there is too much paint flowing out of the cup, you could start again with a smaller hole in the cup, or try using less paint. Let your pendulum swing for less time, too.

FOLLOW-UP

Pendulum painter

After you have made your first paint pattern, try making another by releasing the cup from a different starting point. You could also vary the amount of paint in the cup to see if changing the pendulum's weight makes a difference. On each pattern mark the starting point with a pen, and write down the amount of paint you used.

You can change the way the paint pendulum swings by altering the heights of the two separate parts. First, measure the lengths of each part of your original pendulum. They are shown in the picture on the right. The bottom part is easy to measure, but the top part is more tricky—measure the total distance that the horizontal string hangs down (a).

To make this part longer, loosen it a little. To make (b) longer, untie it and replace it with a longer length of string. Measure the heights each time you change them, and try to get an exact ratio, such as 1:1, 1:3, or 3:4. For

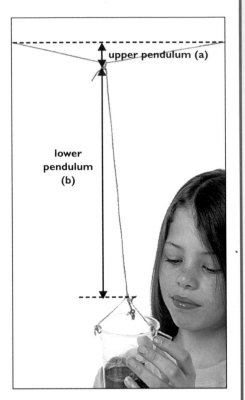

upper pendulum (a)

lower pendulum (b)

each ratio make a new paint pattern, and write the ratio on the paper when the paint is dry. Try varying the cup's starting point or the amount of paint in the cup to see if the pattern changes for each ratio. When the paint trails are dry, pin them on the wall to make a display.

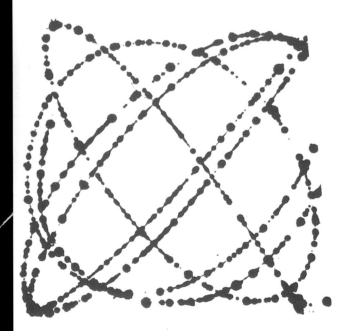

The trail made by your paint pendulum is a record of how the pendulum moved.

ANALYSIS

Pendulums

A pendulum made of two connected parts is called a compound pendulum, and the patterns it makes are called Lissajous patterns. The Lissajous pattern from your first pendulum should have been similar no matter where the cup started or how much paint it contained.

The pattern was probably irregular, since the paint trail slowly covered the paper and did not go over the same path repeatedly. If you changed the lengths of the two parts of the pendulum, it would have made completely different patterns. If you managed to get an exact ratio between the two parts, the cup would have traced a repeating pattern instead of slowly covering the paper with paint. For instance, a ratio of 1:1 should make a circle, 1:2 should make a figure-eight, and so on. The higher the numbers in the ratio, the more complex the pattern becomes. Lissajous patterns depend on the frequencies of the two pendulums. When you change the length of one pendulum, you alter its frequency, and this changes the pattern.

FOUCAULT'S PENDULUM

A simple pendulum always moves between the same two points. The French scientist Léon Foucault used this property to show that Earth rotates. He set a pendulum swinging in a cathedral, and after several hours the pendulum had swung away from its line. Really, it was Earth that had moved, not the path of the pendulum.

Léon Foucault used a pendulum 220 feet (67m) long to show that Earth rotates.

Tick tock, tick tock

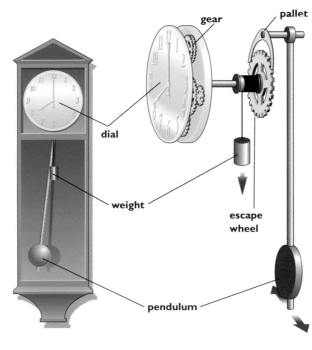

Because a pendulum always swings at the same rate, it can be used to turn the hands of a clock at a constant speed.

In grandfather clocks pendulums control a device called the escape wheel. At the top of the pendulum is a part called a pallet. It has two arms with ends that fit into the teeth on the escape wheel. As the pendulum swings, the pallet rocks back and forth, releasing the escape wheel momentarily and allowing it to turn around by one notch. The escape wheel is connected by gears (toothed wheels) to the hands of the clock,

so they move, too. A falling weight provides the power to keep the pendulum swinging. When the weight has dropped to its lowest point, you have to wind up the clock to raise the weight again.

The length of the pendulum has to be just right to keep accurate time. Remember: The longer a pendulum, the more time it takes to swing. A pendulum that is 39 inches (99cm) long swings once every second. For every 0.001-inch (0.025mm) increase in length, the clock will lose one second per day.

RESONANCE

Pendulums swing with a constant rhythm. If you nudge a pendulum in time with this rhythm, it will swing higher and higher. In this chapter you can find out how to nudge a pendulum and start it swinging without touching it.

Pendulums and all other vibrating objects move back and forth or up and down at a constant rate—their natural frequency. No matter how hard you push a pendulum to start it going, or how far back you pull it, the pendulum will only swing at its natural frequency. If you nudge a pendulum with a rhythm that matches its natural frequency, you can make it swing farther and farther with very little effort. This effect is called resonance.

A swing is a type of pendulum. To make a swing go as high as possible, you have to time your pushes carefully to match the swing's natural frequency. Push too early or too late, and you might bring the swing to a halt rather than making it go farther.

No matter how high this girl swings, she will swing back and forth at the same rate. A swing is a pendulum and has a natural frequency, like all vibrating objects.

Anything that vibrates can resonate. If you hold a violin and sing a note at the natural frequency of one of the strings, the violin will start making sound without being touched. This happens because your voice makes the air vibrate, and the vibrations pass to the string and make it resonate.

Resonance can make objects vibrate so powerfully that they damage themselves. An opera singer with perfect pitch can even shatter a wine glass by singing a note at the glass's natural frequency.

When a washing machine spins, the frequency of the spinner briefly coincides with the natural frequency of the machine and makes it shake, or resonate.

SHAKEN TO BITS

Engineers have to be careful about the natural frequency of the things they build. If a car's body has a natural frequency that matches the engine noise, resonance will make the car vibrate annoyingly when someone drives it.

For the same reason, marching soldiers always break step when they cross a bridge. If they carried on marching in time, the frequency of their steps might match the natural frequency of the bridge and make it resonate. Resonating bridges can shake so violently that people walking over them fall over. Some bridges have even torn themselves apart because of resonance caused by the wind.

Look out for examples of resonance. If you have a washing machine in your house, watch what happens when it starts spinning fast. There might be a point when the whole machine begins to shake. That happens when the frequency of the spinner is the same as the natural frequency of the whole machine. If the natural frequency of the machine happened to match that of the spinner at top speed, the washing machine would soon begin to fall apart. You should find that the spinner reaches the machine's natural frequency for only a very brief moment as it works its way up to maximum speed.

In activity 4 we found that a pendulum's frequency depends only on its length. The two pendulums in the activity on the following pages are the same length, so they will have the same natural frequency. In this activity you can explore how one pendulum can make another resonate by sending vibrations along a connecting string.

Droning on

An old-fashioned stringed instrument called a hurdy-gurdy has a set of strings that are not plucked, bowed, or even touched by the player—and yet they do vibrate and make sound. These strings are called drones. The drones vibrate and make sound when the other strings of the instrument vibrate at their natural frequency. The plucked strings vibrate, making the air around them move and so producing sound. These sound waves pass to the drones and make them resonate, resulting in a rich, whirring sound.

A hurdy-gurdy is played by turning a handle that plucks a set of strings to make them vibrate. The sound the strings make causes separate "drone" strings to vibrate, too.

Twin Pendulums

Goals

1. **Build a pair of resonating pendulums.**
2. **Make a pendulum move without touching it.**

What you will need:

- *metal coat hanger*
- *wire cutters*
- *hole punch*
- *film canisters*
- *metal nuts of the same size to use as weights*
- *string*

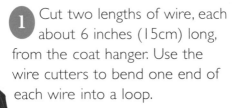

1 Cut two lengths of wire, each about 6 inches (15cm) long, from the coat hanger. Use the wire cutters to bend one end of each wire into a loop.

Safety tip

Take great care when cutting the lengths of wire. Small pieces of wire can fly off and hit you in the eye. Use goggles if you have them. If not, wear glasses or sunglasses. The ends of the wire can be sharp, so take care of your fingers. A hole punch is probably the safest way to make holes in the film canister lids.

2 Ask an adult to make a hole in the middle of each film canister lid. Push the straight ends of the wire through the holes, and bend the wire back so that the canisters can hang from the wire. Make sure that the tops fit onto the canisters properly.

3 Put the same number of nuts in each canister. Put the lids on the canisters.

4 Cut a length of string about 2 feet (61cm) long. Tie it between two chairs or from wall to wall so that it is taught. Hang the wires over the string so that they are about 4 inches (10cm) apart and at equal distances from the center point of the string.

5 Pull back one of the canisters, let go, and allow it to swing. Watch what happens to the other pendulum. If the canisters start to slide together, make the string tighter so that it doesn't sag.

Smooth ride

Automobiles have springs to help them cope with bumpy roads. When a wheel hits a rut in the road, a spring sometimes begins to vibrate at its natural frequency. It can do this for a while, making the ride very bouncy and uncomfortable. To overcome this problem, automobiles are equipped with shock absorbers. One shock-absorbing device is a type of piston. It is a cylinder filled with fluid, which has a disk inside. The disk moves up and down smoothly, absorbing the energy of sudden, juddering jolts and making the ride smoother.

FOLLOW-UP Twin pendulums

Time how long it takes for each pendulum to swing back and forth by itself. This is the pendulum's period. Period is a measure similar to frequency, but it is much easier to measure. Record your results in a table like the one below. Because the wires are the same length, the periods should be the same, too. Swing the pendulums farther, and check whether the periods change—they should be the same.

When you start one canister swinging, watch what happens to the other canister.

Time the period of the first pendulum, and when the second pendulum begins to move, time that, too. Again, record the results in a table.

See what happens when you change the amount of weight in one canister. Do the pendulums still make each other swing when they weigh different amounts?

Repeat the activity with different lengths of wire. First make both wires 1 inch (2.5cm) shorter, then make them both an inch longer. Because the wires are the same length, the periods should be the same, and one pendulum should still set the other swinging. Next, try a different length of wire for each

pendulum. Can you predict what might happen this time?

Now try the activity with three pendulums: two of the same length and one that is longer. Can you predict what will happen if you swing the long pendulum? What do you think might happen if you swing one of the shorter pendulums?

ANALYSIS
Resonance

When the two pendulums were the same length and you set one swinging, you should have noticed that the other pendulum began swinging too. That is because the pendulums had the same period (they took the same time to complete a swing), which means they also had the same natural frequency. As the first pendulum swung, it transmitted vibrations through the string to the second pendulum. These vibrations nudged the second pendulum at its natural frequency, making it resonate. The weight in the canisters should

have made no difference—a pendulum's frequency depends on its length, not its weight.

If you changed the lengths of the pendulums equally, they would still have made each other swing. However, if you made one shorter or longer than the other, the first pendulum would have swung on its own. If you set up three pendulums, you would have found that the short pendulums made each other resonate (because they had the same period), but not the long one. Likewise, the long pendulum would have swung on its own if you pushed it first.

ACTIVITY 6
BUILDING BRIDGES

Bridges have to support their own weight as well as the weight of traffic traveling over them. Engineers use supports, arches, and cables to design bridges that balance these downward forces with upward or inward forces.

The first bridges that people used were made by simply laying fallen trees over streams. Later, people began to make better, flatter bridges out of planks of wood or slabs of stone. All these early bridges worked in the same way. They were beam bridges: flat, solid structures supported at each end where the bridge rests on the ground.

Beam bridges have limitations. If a beam bridge is too long, it bends and shakes as you walk across it. One solution to this problem is to put extra supports under the bridge at intervals. They can be supporting towers called piers, which stand in the river, or floating supports called pontoons. A beam bridge with piers or pontoons is really a series of shorter bridges joined together. Although it is better than a single, unsupported beam, it still has drawbacks. Piers and pontoons get in the way of boats, for example, and bridges across deep ravines are often too high up for piers to support them.

ADMIRABLE ARCHES

A beam bridge cannot support much weight before it starts to bend. One way around this problem is to build an arch-shaped bridge or a beam bridge with an arch beneath. The force pushing down on an arch is carried around and downward to where the arch meets the ground. This spreads the load across the whole bridge, so an arch can support much more weight than a beam without bending.

A suspension bridge also distributes weight more evenly than a beam bridge. Suspension bridges hang from two enormous cables slung across tall towers. A force pushing down on the center of the bridge makes the road pull on small vertical cables.

The Tsing Ma Bridge in Hong Kong is one of the world's longest suspension bridges. The cables holding it up are 3.63 feet (1.1 m) thick.

They, in turn, pull on the main cables, which transfer the force to the towers. The main cables also run from the tops of the towers to the ground at either end of the bridge, where they are anchored down by gigantic blocks of concrete.

ACTIVITY

Bend and Bow

Goals

1. **Build a beam bridge.**
2. **Test the strength of your beam bridge.**

What you will need:

- *ruler*
- *pencil*
- *cardboard*
- *scissors*
- *enough heavy books to make two piles of the same height*
- *camera film canisters*
- *metal washers or coins to use as weights*

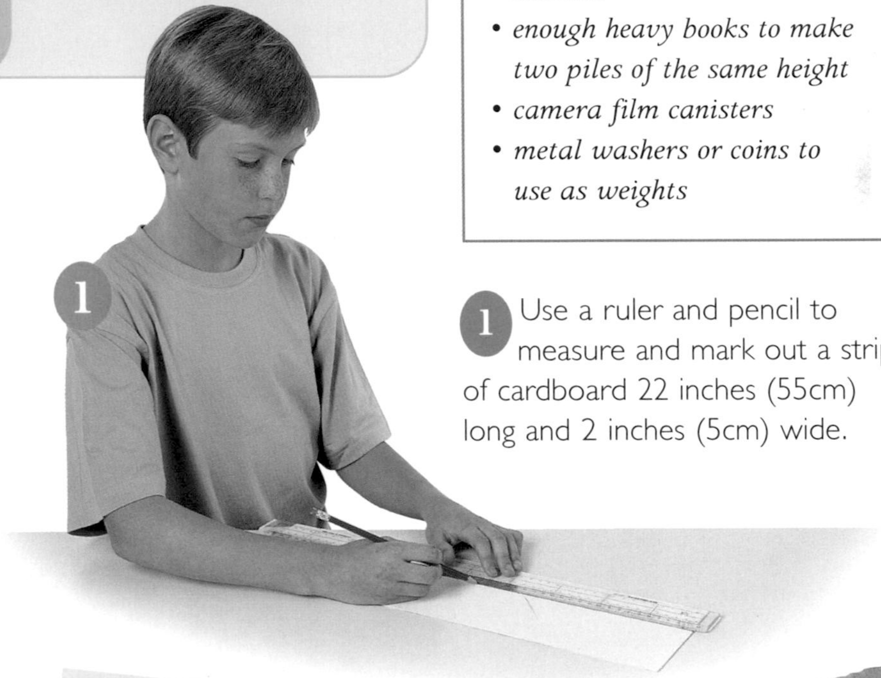

1 Use a ruler and pencil to measure and mark out a strip of cardboard 22 inches (55cm) long and 2 inches (5cm) wide.

2 Cut out the cardboard strip. Use a ruler to find the halfway point along one long side, and mark this point with the pencil.

Galloping Gertie

Sometimes bridge designers make serious mistakes. That happened in 1940, when the Tacoma Narrows Bridge in Washington State collapsed. The suspension bridge, built across a stretch of water called the Narrows of Puget Sound, was nicknamed "Galloping Gertie" because of the way it used to swing and flex. The designers had not allowed for the winds that blew up the Narrows. On November 7 the bridge twisted so much in the wind that the structure could take no more, and the bridge collapsed into the water, taking with it a small dog, abandoned in a car.

Better to bend

Flying through turbulence can be a frightening experience. The wing tips of an airplane move up and down many feet in the bumpy air, which is exactly what they are designed to do. If designers tried to build wings that did not bend, they would have to be impossibly thick and heavy. It is much better to allow the structure to bend. Next time you are in an airplane, compare the position of the wings before takeoff with their position once the plane is in the air. Bridges are also designed to sway and bend a little in the wind.

3 Make two piles of books 18 inches (45cm) apart. Place the cardboard strip between the books to make a bridge.

4 Place the canister on the midway point of the bridge. Put a weight in the canister, and measure how much the bridge sags—the distance from the table to the center of the bridge.

5 Keep adding weights until the bridge collapses or touches the ground. Take a measurement each time you add a weight.

FOLLOW-UP Bend and bow

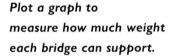

Use your measurements of how much the beam bridge bends to draw a graph. Plot the number of weights in the canister along one axis and the distance from the bridge to the tabletop along the other. This gap will become smaller as the bridge sags more.

Repeat the experiment with a cardboard arch placed under the bridge, as in the photo below. This arched support makes a big difference in the strength of the bridge. Test the strength of the second bridge with the weights, and plot the results on your graph. How do the two graphs compare? Which bridge can hold the most weight?

Another way to strengthen your bridge is to make a pair of reinforcements. Take two strips of cardboard the same length as the bridge, each 1 inch (2.5cm) wide. Fold them twice lengthways so

Make an arch support for your bridge. See if this makes the bridge stronger.

that they form a triangle, and tape them. Now tape them under the sides of the bridge, pointed end down. How much weight can this bridge hold compared to the others?

Try to think of other ways to strengthen your cardboard bridge, such as folding the cardboard strip into a square-ended tube or bending it into a corrugated sheet. Test each design with your weights.

The world's largest and most powerful bridges are suspension bridges and cantilever bridges. They both work by spreading out the load they carry and transferring forces to their foundations or to anchors.

Suspension bridges can span more than a mile to carry traffic across bays or to islands.

Cantilever bridges can hold huge weights, so they are often used for railroads. Unlike suspension bridges, cantilever

Plot a graph to measure how much weight each bridge can support.

bridges are constructed from rigid steel struts rather than flexible cables. Can you think of a way to build a cantilever or suspension bridge from cardboard and string?

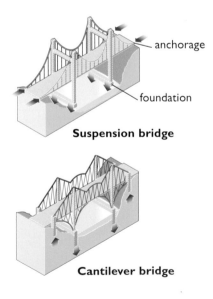

Suspension bridge — anchorage, foundation

Suspension bridge

Cantilever bridge

The red arrows show where forces act as each bridge pushes down on to its foundations and pulls at its anchors on land.

ANALYSIS
Building bridges

In your beam bridge the weight was supported at each end where the strip was held between books. The bridge could not hold much weight because it bent too easily. Reinforcing it with triangular beams increased how much weight it could carry by helping to spread the load, but the downward force was still supported in the same way.

Arch bridges work differently. The force produced by a weight on the bridge spreads across the bridge and transfers to the ground diagonally at each end of the arch. This enables the arch to hold much more weight than a beam. While the beam bridge bent under its load, the arch bridge was compressed (see box below).

The ends of an arch bridge not only push downward, but also push outward. The ends of your arch were supported by the piles of books, but without them the arch would have spread out and collapsed. This limitation means that arch bridges can only be built where there is firm ground at either side.

Most of the weight carried by a suspension bridge is not held by the towers but by the cable anchors at either end. Downward force on the bridge tightens the cables, making them pull at their anchors. This force is called tension (see box below). Cantilever bridges spread their load through forces of tension in the upper beams and compression in the lower ones.

Feel the forces

Four different forces act on the structure of a bridge: compression, tension, bending, and twisting. Engineers try to work out how their bridge will respond to each of these forces. You can apply similar forces to a plastic ruler.

1) compression

2) tension

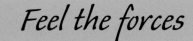

In some places the structure of a bridge will be compressed. Push the two ends of the ruler together to compress it (**1**). Other parts of the bridge will be in tension. You can create tension by pulling the ruler from each end (**2**).

Hold the ruler in front of you so that the measuring edge is facing you. Try to bend it up

3) bending

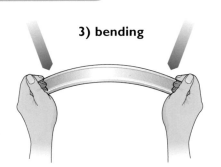

and down. It should be almost impossible to bend in this position. Now hold it with the measuring edge facing up. Bend it up and down again. It should be much easier this time (**3**).

Some parts of a bridge will twist. Turn the ends of the ruler in opposite directions to see what happens when the structure twists (**4**).

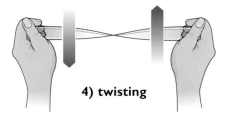

4) twisting

ACTIVITY 7
UP THE RAMP

Many machines have been invented to make it easier to lift heavy objects. Some of the most effective are surprisingly simple and are used all around us. Ramps, for example, are simple machines.

This skateboarder uses a ramp to help him go fast enough to perform airborne tricks.

We use the word machine to describe many of the things we use in daily life. Washing machines, cars, lawnmowers, and computers are all machines. But many of the machines we use are much simpler than that. A screw, a zipper, and an ax, for example, are all types of a simple machine called an inclined plane, or ramp. Ramps allow us to use less effort to accomplish more work.

It takes a certain amount of effort to lift an object to a particular height. Effort can come from either your muscles or from a complex machine, like an elevator. The amount of effort that it takes to lift an object depends on two things: the weight of the object and the distance it has to be moved.

When you lift a heavy stone onto a table, for example, your muscles provide the effort. The higher the table and the heavier the stone, the more your muscles must strain to move the stone. But if you could push or pull the stone up a ramp, it would be easier. That is because a ramp decreases the amount of effort it takes to move an object by increasing the distance the object has to travel. This allows the object to be moved using less effort, but over a longer distance. This is easiest to understand by looking at the following example.

Climbing a hill by the steepest route requires the most effort, but the distance that you have to cover is shortest. Climbing up the same hill by the gentlest slope requires the least effort, but the distance is greatest. The effort you use is the same in either case and equals the effort (the force you exert to walk) multiplied by the distance over which you maintain the effort (the path).

So what you gain in effort, you pay in distance. This is a basic rule that is obeyed by many mechanical devices, and it is the reason why the ramp works: it reduces the effort needed to raise an object by increasing the distance that it moves.

Ramps have many practical uses in everyday life. Here, cars and trucks in Calagari, Italy, use a ramp to help them leave and enter a ferryboat.

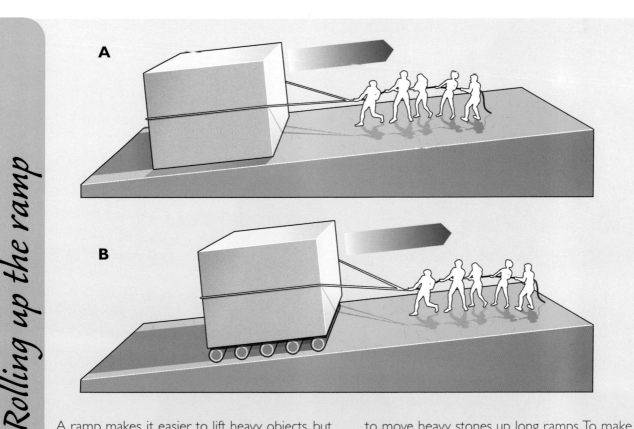

Rolling up the ramp

A ramp makes it easier to lift heavy objects, but one problem with using a ramp is friction. Any object that is pulled up a ramp will rub against it, creating friction (A). This rubbing makes it harder to pull the object—a bigger force is needed. When the Egyptians built the pyramids, they had to move heavy stones up long ramps. To make the stones easier to pull, the surface of the ramp was covered in logs (B) or layers of wet gravel and sand. As the stones moved over these layers, the grains slid and rolled, reducing friction. Today, we would probably use wheels to reduce the friction.

Building a Ramp

Goals

1. **Learn why less force is needed to lift a load when a ramp is used.**
2. **Understand the idea of mechanical advantage.**

What you will need:

- hole punch
- film canister
- rubber bands or piece of elastic
- coins or metal nuts
- ruler
- books
- wooden board or piece of plastic 2 feet (61cm) long

1 Start by making a small hole in the lid of the film canister with a hole punch. Thread the elastic through the hole, and tie a knot in it so that it does not slip out.

A round plane

A screw uses a type of ramp to help it to move through wood. It would be very difficult to push a piece of metal directly into the wood. A screw has a thread that spirals around it from one end to the other. When someone turns the screw with a screwdriver, the thread acts like a ramp, moving forward (into the wood) with a greater force than is used to turn it.

2 Put some coins or weights in the bottom half of the canister, and click the lid back on.

Safety tip

If you don't have a hole punch, ask an adult to make a hole in the lid.

Troubleshooting

What if the elastic doesn't stretch enough to measure?

Some types of elastic are not very stretchy. If your elastic does not stretch, or only stretches a little bit, try using a rubber band instead. Cut the rubber band so that it makes one long piece. To keep it from pulling through the hole, tie one end around a toothpick, then push the other end through the hole in the lid.

3 Measure the length of the elastic without stretching it.

4 Use the elastic to slowly lift the weight up to the height of a stack of books. Measure the length of the elastic when it is at the height of the top book.

5 Now make a smooth ramp up to the books with the wooden or plastic board. Fix the ramp with clay at the bottom to keep it from sliding.

6 Use the elastic to pull the weight slowly up to the top of the ramp. Measure the length of the elastic as it pulls the weight.

FOLLOW-UP Building a ramp

One way to test how well your ramp works is to repeat the activity with the ramp set at different angles. You will need a different length of ramp for each angle. Use a ramp made of thick cardboard. Start with the ramp at a shallow angle, and gradually cut the ramp shorter so that the angle becomes steeper. Use a

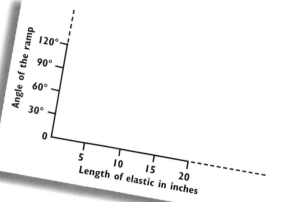

protractor to measure the angle of each ramp that you use.

Plot a graph of ramp angle against the length of the stretched elastic. It will show you the force needed to raise the load at each angle—the longer the stretch in the elastic, the bigger the force.

You would be able to lift the load with less force if you could reduce the friction between the ramp and the load. Try using different materials to reduce the friction. For example, you could sprinkle salt, talcum powder, or oil on the ramp.

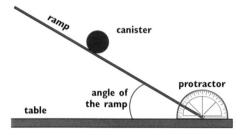

Measure the length of the elastic as you drag the load over the friction-reducing materials.

Another way to reduce friction is by using rollers. Use drinking straws cut into lengths of about 2 inches (1 cm) to make rollers. Place the straws between a piece of cardboard and the ramp. Put the load on top of the cardboard, and pull it up the ramp as before. Once again, draw a graph plotting the results. Try using rollers

made from other materials as well.

Heavy weights are sometimes lifted with the help of a second weight called a counterweight. Elevators usually have a counterweight attached to the other end of the lifting cable. When the elevator moves up, the counterweight moves down.

You could make a counterweight to use in this activity by fastening a second film canister filled with weights to the opposite end of the elastic. Allow the counterweight to hang down over the back of the book. Put the back of the book over the edge of a table so that the counterweight can fall. Draw graphs of the amount of stretch at each ramp angle as you did before.

ANALYSIS
Up the ramp

In this activity you should have found that it takes less force, or effort, to push or pull an object up a ramp than it does to lift the object straight up. The saving in effort that you gain from using a ramp is called mechanical advantage. In general, the longer the ramp is, the less effort it takes to move an object up it, and the more mechanical advantage you gain.

The downside of using a ramp is that it takes longer to move the object because you have to move the object over a greater distance. But if the object is too heavy to lift straight up, then a ramp is a good alternative. Remember this the next time you want to move a heavy object.

You can find ramps in some unexpected places. A zipper works by pushing together two rows of teeth that interlock to make a strong fastening. Inside the slide (the part that moves up and down) is a triangular wedge. To zip together, the teeth move down either side of the wedge and are pushed together. The wedge acts like two ramps that meet at one end. To unzip, another wedge pushes the teeth apart when the slide is moved in the opposite direction.

Archimedes' screw

The thread of a screw provides mechanical advantage in the same way as a ramp. A screw can produce a large mechanical advantage because it turns around a greater distance than it moves forward. This means that it moves forward with greater force than is used to turn it.

In ancient times people used the Archimedes' screw (left) to lift water from rivers or gorges into fields. Every time the screw turns, it lifts the water a little higher up inside a tube. The Archimedes' screw was turned by a person using a handle on the end of the screw. This was a slow way of raising water, but it was easier than lifting or carrying the water straight up in buckets.

Some archaeologists believe that a series of Archimedes' screws may once have been used to raise water up to the Hanging Gardens of Babylon in ancient Iraq, one of the wonders of the ancient world. The gardens were built on terraces high above the city and high above the nearest water.

The Archimedes' screw is still used today in many industries. For heavy commercial use a motor turns the screw very quickly.

An Archimedes' screw is used to move pellets of plastic mixed with water through a recycling plant.

EASIER WITH A LEVER

We use many machines to make our lives easier. One of the simplest machines is the lever, which people have used since prehistoric times. Levers magnify forces, making it easier to move a load.

We saw in the last experiment that a ramp is a simple machine. Another simple machine that people have used to move all types of loads for thousands of years is the lever. Levers work by either increasing force or increasing a movement. A lever moves around a fixed point called a fulcrum that gives the lever its power. The simplest lever is a single length of rigid material, like a pole or a pipe. Other levers can be more complicated, but they all work in the same way.

Imagine moving a boulder by using a wooden pole as a lever. You first push one end of the pole under the boulder and then place a brick beneath

These Romanian loggers are using long wooden poles as levers to roll heavy logs onto a cart.

the lever, close to the boulder. The brick acts as a fulcrum. You then push down on the end of the pole farthest from the boulder. Because the fulcrum is closer to the boulder than it is to you, the big movement of the lever at your end makes a small movement under the boulder, but it makes the force bigger. The increase in force is enough to raise a boulder that you could not lift by hand. The object that a lever lifts is called the load, and the force you use to move the lever is called the effort.

THREE TYPES OF LEVER

There are three types of levers that help us to move loads. They work in different ways.

Type one
The fulcrum (the green triangle) is between the load (the blue brick) and the effort (where the person pushes down—the red arrow). A type-one lever magnifies force.

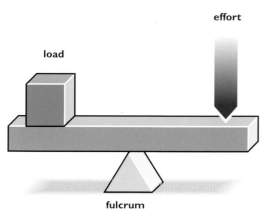

A claw hammer, used to pull nails out of wood, is a type-one lever. Effort is applied at the top of the handle. The hammer head (claw) is the fulcrum, and the nail is the load. A pair of scissors is made of two type-one levers working together. The point where the two blades cross is the fulcrum. They are called compound type-one levers.

Type two
In a type-two lever the load is between the fulcrum and the effort. Imagine we rearranged the type-one lever. This time the end of the lever is resting on the fulcrum, while the blue block is halfway down the lever. The person lifting the lever (effort) is at the opposite end from the fulcrum. Because the large movement of the effort moves the load a shorter distance, the force is magnified. A wheelbarrow is an example of a simple type-two lever.

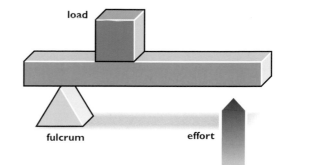

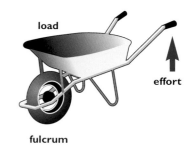

Nutcrackers are an example of two type-two levers working together. The hinge is the fulcrum, and the nut is the load. Such levers are compound type-two levers.

Type three
A type-three lever magnifies movement, not force. If we rearrange our lever once again, we can make a type-three lever. Imagine that one end of the lever rests on the fulcrum as before. The load is at the other end of the lever. The person applying the effort is between the fulcrum and the load. The movement of the effort makes an even bigger movement of the load. The movement is magnified, but

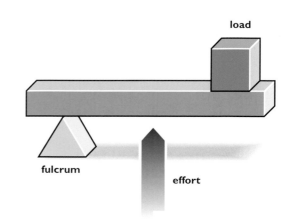

the force is reduced. This type of lever is ideal for tools where delicate grip and control are needed. Tweezers are compound type-three levers.

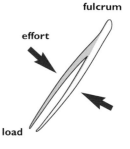

Making a lever

ACTIVITY

Goals

1. Make a simple type-one lever.
2. Explore how the lever magnifies force.

What you will need:

- 2 1-foot (30cm) rulers
- 24 matchsticks
- tape
- four books
- 2 film canisters
- coins or metal nuts
- modeling clay

Improvised lever

In 1947 Chuck Yeager became the first person to travel faster than sound. The day before his historic flight Yeager was thrown from his horse as he rode through the desert. With broken ribs he found it impossible to close his airplane's hatch—until he lashed a broom handle to it, making a long lever.

1 Draw lines on one of the rulers at 1-inch (2.5cm) intervals. Then tape pairs of matchsticks next to each mark. Each pair of matchsticks should be about 0.13 inch (3mm) apart. The matchsticks will keep the lever from slipping.

2 Now use the second ruler to make a platform for the lever to rest on. Wedge the ruler between four heavy books. Leave about 12 inches (30cm) of the middle of the ruler uncovered. The point where the lever balances on this ruler will be the fulcrum.

3 Take two blobs of modeling clay of the same size. Place a piece of modeling clay on the base of each film canister. Stick one canister to each end of the lever on the matchstick-free side.

4 Use the coins or metal nuts as weights. Put two weights in one of the canisters and four in the other. You are going to try to raise the heavier weight (the load) with the lighter weight (the effort), using your lever to magnify the effort.

5 Place the lever centrally on the supporting ruler. It won't balance at first, so adjust the position of the lighter weight until the lever balances. Write down the position of the fulcrum (where the rulers touch) and the distances between the fulcrum and the weights. Repeat the activity, each time moving the lever up one matchstick-notch on the lever.

Troubleshooting

What if the film canisters keep falling off the lever each time I lift it up to move it?

Use a larger piece of modeling clay to keep the canisters in place, but make sure you use the same size under each canister. Otherwise the weight of the clay would affect the experiment. If you are worried that one blob is heavier than the other, weigh them on kitchen scales first.

FOLLOW-UP Making a lever

Draw a graph showing the distance from the heavier weight (load) to the fulcrum against the distance from the small weight (effort) to the fulcrum at the points when the two weights balanced (see below).

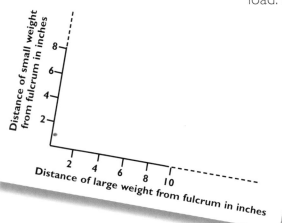

Plot your results on a graph like this one, and draw a line to link up all the points.

The lever in this first activity is a type-one lever. Try to make a type-two lever. This time you will apply the effort by pulling on a length of elastic instead of using a canister full of weights.

Rest one end of the lever on the fixed ruler (the fixed ruler is the fulcrum). Now put a weight on top of the lever close to the fulcrum. Take a length of elastic with a loop tied at one end. Put the loop over the lever so that you can pull on it

to raise the load (see picture). Start with the elastic close to the load, and gently lift the lever. Measure how much the elastic stretches. To do this, make a mark at the top and bottom of the elastic, and measure the distance between the two before and after you lift the load. Now move the elastic one matchstick notch farther from the load, and repeat the lifting and measuring. Keep on doing this until you reach the end of the lever farthest from the fulcrum. Plot a graph of the amount the elastic stretches against the distance of the elastic from the load. The amount of stretch in the elastic is a measure of the effort you need to apply to lift the load at each stage.

What does the new graph tell you about the way a type-two lever works? Look at the small distance the load moves compared to the effort in this type of lever.

Now rearrange the fulcrum, load, and effort to make a type-three lever. The fulcrum stays as it was for the type-two lever but the load should be at the opposite end of the lever from the fulcrum. The elastic should be looped around the lever between the fulcrum and the load. Start with the elastic close to the fulcrum, and gradually move out toward the load.

Plot a graph of the amount the elastic stretches against the distance from the load. Compare the graph with the graph for the type-two lever. Note how far the load moves compared to the effort. Remember that a type-three lever magnifies movement and not force.

Find out how much effort you need to lift the load. Do this by measuring how much the piece of elastic stretches.

ANALYSIS
Easier with a lever

A wheelbarrow is a type of lever. This trader in Laos is using a wheelbarrow to carry her heavy produce to market.

The position of the fulcrum in relation to the effort and the load was crucial in all the levers that you made. That should have shown up on your graphs. The farther the effort was from the fulcrum, the easier it was to move the load.

When you used elastic to lift the type-two lever, you should have found that the farther the elastic was from the fulcrum, the less the elastic stretched—less effort was required. When it was closer to the fulcrum, the elastic stretched more, showing that greater effort was needed to move the load.

You might also have realized that as the type-one or type-two lever becomes longer, it gets easier to lift a load. But if the lever gets too long, it snaps under pressure.

CLEVER LEVERS

Type-one and type-two levers convert a small effort into a larger force to move a load. In the first two levers you made, you will have seen that the effort moves the lever a large distance, but the load does not move as far. The energy of your effort is concentrated by the fulcrum into a smaller movement, which magnifies the lifting force exerted on the load.

A type-three lever works differently. With the load on one side of the effort and the fulcrum on the other, the effort required to move the load must be greater—the fulcrum does not magnify the effort. You will have noticed that the piece of elastic stretched more the farther you moved away from the load and the closer you got to the fulcrum.

The advantage of a type-three lever is that you can exert force with great control. This is very useful when you undertake delicate tasks, such as eating with chopsticks or using tweezers to grip something tiny.

LOOK OUT FOR LEVERS

Look around you at everyday machines (and remember that machines can be very simple). See how many levers you can spot. Can you figure out what type each one is? Some complicated machines contain more than one lever. Next time you see a building site, take a look at the way the machines work, or watch workmen repairing a sidewalk or highway. What do they use to lift paving slabs? Can you see where the fulcrum is and how it affects the effort and the load?

Some of the biggest levers can be found on-board ships. Everything on a ship seems to be larger than life, even the tools that are used to make repairs. Huge wrenches, many feet long, act as levers to loosen the massive nuts that hold the ship's engine together.

THE BIG PULL

To lift really enormous weights, you need a device called a pulley. Pulleys are simple machines that reduce the effort needed to move a load. Here we explore how pulleys change forces so that they work in our favor.

We all know that pulling something down is easier than lifting it up. When you pull down, your whole body can help you pull; but when you lift up, you use mostly the muscles in your arms.

A pulley is a simple machine that converts the easier downward pull into an upward lift, so that a heavy load can be raised with less effort. The amount of decrease in effort is called the mechanical advantage.

The grooved pulley wheel used with ropes is called a sheave. A single, fixed pulley, consisting of one sheave mounted in a block and fixed in place (see photo), simply changes the direction of force.

If you run a rope from a load through two pulleys, one of which is attached to a beam overhead, the pulleys will magnify your pulling force. A pulley system that uses more than one pulley is called a compound pulley or

Heavy-duty pulleys consist of a wheel mounted in a steel housing. The load hangs from a hook.

block and tackle. A compound pulley is made up of two pulleys and multiplies your pulling force by two. In other words, this pulley has a mechanical advantage of two. However, you can move the load only half the distance for the same amount of pulling effort as with a single pulley.

There are limits to the number of pulleys that a compound pulley can contain. As more pulleys are added, more energy is lost due to friction where the rope moves over the pulley wheels. Additional pulleys also add to the total weight of the load.

Pulleys are found in many places in everyday life, wherever loads need to be moved. Construction sites and warehouses are good places to see pulleys in action. In particular look for the huge, complex tower cranes used in building construction, which rely on complicated compound pulley systems.

PULLEYS AND MECHANICAL ADVANTAGE

The diagrams below show how different pulley systems work. Bear in mind that in order to gain the full mechanical advantage from each system, you should pull directly downward on the rope so no effort is wasted pulling out to the side.

Diagram 1

There is no pulley in this diagram. If you lift the load by pulling up at (**A**), you pull all the load's weight by yourself. There is no mechanical advantage.

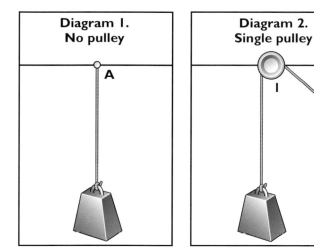

Giant pulleys are used to drive the cable-car system in San Francisco. Instead of a person pulling on the metal cables, a series of engines is used to pull the cables and drag the cars up the city's hills.

Diagram 4

Here, two fixed pulleys (**3** and **4**) are attached to the beam. The load is attached to two free pulleys (**1** and **2**), which are mounted on the same axle. The rope is attached to the beam, looped around pulley (**1**), up and around pulley (**3**), down around pulley (**2**), then over pulley (**4**). When the rope is pulled down at (**A**), all four pulleys lift the load at the same time. The lifting effort is multiplied by four. Only a quarter of the effort used in Diagram 2 is needed to lift the load, but the rope must be pulled four times as far. This is a mechanical advantage of four. To calculate the mechanical advantage easily, count the strands of rope that pull up on the free pulley (do not count those that are not pulling up).

Diagram 2

Now the rope passes through a fixed pulley wheel (**1**) and then down to the person pulling. As the person pulls the rope at (**A**), the pulley changes the direction of the force, pulling the load upward. There is still no gain in mechanical advantage, but the change in the direction of force makes the work easier.

Diagram 3

A double pulley system. The load is directly attached to the free pulley (**1**), and the fixed pulley (**2**) is attached to the beam. As the rope is pulled down at (**A**), the load is pulled up by both pulleys at the same time so that the pulling effort is doubled. It takes only half the effort to lift the load, but the rope must be pulled twice as far. This is a mechanical advantage of two.

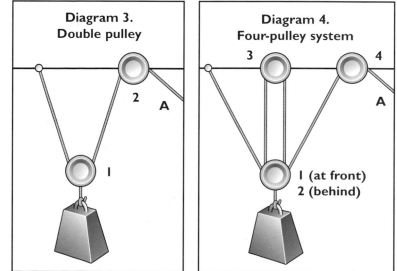

Pulling with a Pulley

ACTIVITY

Goals

1. **Make a pulley system**
2. **Reduce the force needed to lift a load.**

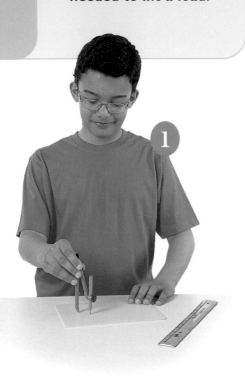

What you will need:

- compass
- pencils
- sheet of thick cardboard
- glue
- 2 small plastic cups
- hole punch
- string
- wooden dowel
- 2 chairs
- coins or metal washers/nuts

1 Start by making the pulley wheel. Use a compass to draw three circles on thick cardboard. Two of the circles should have a diameter of 2 inches (5cm), so set your compass so that the distance between the pencil and the point is 1 inch (2.5cm). The other circle should be 1.75 inches (4.4cm) wide—move your compass apart 0.87 inches (2cm).

2 Now glue the circles together, with the small circle sandwiched between the two larger ones. Put a weight on top of the wheel as it dries so that it bonds well. If you cannot find thick cardboard, use double thickness of thin cardboard.

3 Ask an adult to help you make a hole big enough for a pencil through the center of the wheel. Push a pencil through the hole.

Pulled free

Off-road vehicles can sometimes get stuck in mud. That is why many of them are equipped with a built-in winch. When it is obvious that wheels alone cannot move the vehicle, the driver takes the cable from the winch and fastens it to a tree. The winch, driven by the vehicle's own engine, uses a compound-pulley system to haul the stuck vehicle free.

4 Make two holes near the top of each plastic cup, and tie a short piece of string between the holes.

5 Use two lengths of string to hang the pulley from the dowel. Balance the dowel between two chairs so it is off the ground. Place a long piece of string over the pulley wheel so that it hangs down on both sides, and tie one cup to one end of the string.

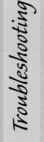

Safety tip

Cutting thick cardboard can be difficult. If you have any problems doing it, ask an adult to help you. Use a hole punch to make holes in the cups safely.

6 Place a few coins or weights in the cup, and pull down on the string. Notice how much effort it takes to lift the weight.

Troubleshooting

What should I do if the pulley keeps getting stuck and does not move freely?

If the pulley wheel does not move smoothly, you might have to make the pencil hole a little bigger so that the pencil can turn around easily.

7 Now tie the second cup to the other end of the string. Place several weights in one of the cups. Add weights to the other cup until the first cup rises. Write down the number of coins in each cup.

FOLLOW-UP Pulling with a pulley

Now that you have studied simple pulleys, you can make a compound pulley. First, make a second pulley just like the one in the main activity.

Tie one cup to the pencil of the second pulley as shown in the picture here. Then tie one end of a long piece of string to the dowel. Loop the string down and around the unfixed pulley, then up and over the fixed pulley. Tie a second cup onto the end of the string.

Draw up a table with two columns. Put four weights in the cup that is attached to the unfixed pulley, and write the number in the first column. These weights are the load. Now add weights, one at a time, to the other cup until the first cup rises. Write the number of weights in the second cup in the next column. This is the amount of effort it takes to lift the load.

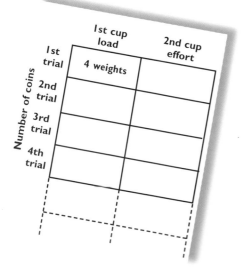

	1st cup load	2nd cup effort
1st trial	4 weights	
2nd trial		
3rd trial		
4th trial		

Number of coins

Repeat the experiment, adding an extra weight to the first cup each time. Write down your results. Do you notice anything interesting about the way the numbers in both columns go up?

You can increase the mechanical advantage even further by adding more pulleys to the system. Make two more pulley wheels, and slide them onto the pencils next to the original wheels so that there are two pulley wheels on each pencil. Tie the pencils to the dowel exactly as before. Tie one cup to the pencil of the unfixed pulley. Tie one end of a long piece of string to the dowel, and loop the string over the pulleys as shown in the diagram. Then tie a second cup to the end of the string. Repeat the experiments you tried

with the original two-pulley system, and draw up a chart recording how many weights were needed to lift the cup.

Can you figure out the mechanical advantage of this pulley system?

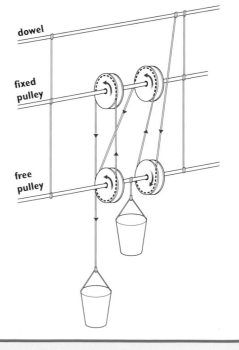

dowel

fixed pulley

free pulley

ANALYSIS

The big pull

After building the pulleys in these activities, you should have a much better idea of how single-pulley and compound-pulley systems work.

The single pulley did not add mechanical advantage. You needed to put at least the same number of coins in the second cup in order to raise the first cup. In fact, you probably needed more coins in the second cup since some of the weight is needed to overcome friction between the pencil and the strings.

Single pulleys are very useful tools for changing the direction of pull so that a heavy weight can be raised by pulling down rather than by lifting up. As we found in the introduction, pulling down is easier than lifting up. However, a single pulley does not add any mechanical advantage and so does not reduce the effort needed to lift the load.

The two-pulley system should have led to a very different result. You should have found that you made the weighted cup rise by adding only half the amount of weight to the empty cup (again, making allowances for friction). That is a mechanical advantage of two. If you made the four-pulley system shown in the diagram, you would have discovered that you needed to add only one-quarter of the weight

🔴 *Pulleys enable these hikers to winch themselves and their equipment across a river gorge.*

to make the first cup rise—a mechanical advantage of four.

WHAT HAPPENED?

Each time you added weights to the empty cup, they created a force, or effort. The force pulled the string and lifted the load in the weighted cup. The reason for the difference in the amount of effort needed with a single pulley and with a compound pulley is that the compound pulley magnifies the force and creates a mechanical advantage, so the weight can be lifted more easily.

You may have noticed that the distance the cup moved down was roughly double the distance that the other cup rose in the two-pulley system. This demonstrates a relationship between distance and effort that is true for all simple machines: The cost of using less effort is that the load moves a shorter distance than the effort. The effort is doubled by using the two pulleys, but the distance the load rises is half the distance it moves on a single pulley.

The next time you are passing a construction site or a dockyard where cranes are in use, look out for pulley systems. Try to find where the effort is being put in, how many pulleys are in each system, and how much mechanical advantage is gained.

ACTIVITY 10
FLOATING

When an object bobs on the surface of a liquid or floats in a gas, it is because the liquid or gas pushes up against it. In this activity we find out why some objects sink and some float.

Objects only float in water if they have a lower density than the water. A diver can control his or her density with an air-filled vest called a buoyancy-control device.

or displaces. The amount of water an object displaces depends on its density—a measure of the amount of matter in an object (mass), compared to its volume (size).

For an object to float in water, its density needs to be less than the density of water. Otherwise the water cannot provide enough upthrust to support the object.

The easiest way to understand how an object's density affects upthrust is to try the following experiment. Roll a lump of modeling clay into a ball, and put it into a container of water. The modeling clay will sink (**1**) because it is denser than water. Next, make the same lump of modeling clay into a boat shape, and put it back on the water. This time it should float (**2**). Although the modeling

Why do objects seem to get lighter when they are in water? It is because the water is pushing up against the object, supporting it. This supporting force is called upthrust. The upthrust is equal to the weight of water the object pushes away,

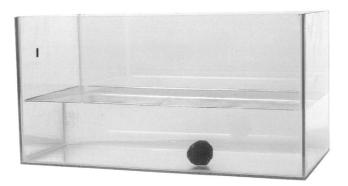

The hot air in these balloons is less dense than the surrounding cold air, so the balloons rise into the sky.

against it. Archimedes found that the more water that is displaced by an object, the larger the force of the upthrust.

Objects can float in gases as well as in liquids. Helium-filled balloons float in air because helium is a very light gas—much less dense than air. Helium balloons are used to carry scientific equipment up into the atmosphere to take readings of air pollution. Even with the balloon material and the equipment, the complete flying machine is less dense than the same volume of air. Hot-air balloons float because the air inside them expands, becoming less dense as it gets warmer. The balloon pilot fires a burner to heat the air in the balloon. If the air cools, it becomes more dense, and the balloon will fall.

clay is more dense than water, the boat is hollow—it is a combination of modeling clay and air, which together are less dense than water. Now try putting marbles into your boat. This time the combined density of the boat and the marbles is greater than that of the water, and the boat will sink.

BATHTIME BRAINWAVE

Greek scientist Archimedes (287–212 B.C.) discovered that the upthrust force of water on a floating or immersed object is equal to the weight of water displaced by the object. Archimedes is said to have made this discovery after stepping into the bath and noticing the water overflow. He was so excited by his finding that he ran out of the public baths naked and shouting "Eureka!" which means "I've got it!" He used the discovery to prove that the king had been swindled by a goldsmith who had not used enough gold to make the king's crown.

Archimedes realized that when an object floats in water, it is held by two forces. The weight of the object pulls it down, while the water pushes up

How low can it go?

A heavy ship floats because it displaces an amount of water that is as heavy as the ship itself (**1**). This creates upthrust, the force that keeps the ship afloat.

However, if a ship is overloaded (**2**), the ship and its load become too heavy to float—they are too dense. The ship may sink. All ships have a mark on their side that tells the captain how low the ship can float in the water. This mark is called the Plimsoll line.

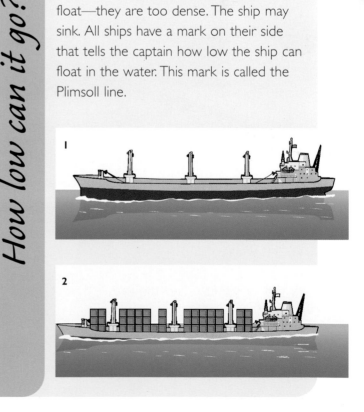

Weighing Water

Goals

1. **Show that an object placed in water pushes aside some of the water.**
2. **Compare the weight of the displaced water and the weight of the object.**

What you will need:

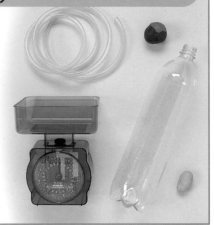

- *modeling clay*
- *weighing scales with container or a separate bowl*
- *large plastic soda bottle*
- *plastic tubing*

Safety tip

Be careful when making holes in the plastic container—it is best to ask an adult to make the holes in the container for you.

1 Place the empty container on the scale, and set the scale to read zero. Take a large piece of clay, and weigh it.

2 Ask an adult to cut the top off a large plastic soda bottle and make a hole in the side just above halfway up. Place a piece of plastic tubing through the hole.

3 Place a piece of modeling clay around the edge of the hole where the tubing enters the bottle. It prevents water from leaking out around the edges.

Double density

Submarines move up and down in the water by changing their density. To do this, they are built with two hulls, one inside the other. The main hull is always filled with air, and it is the part of the submarine that contains the crew, engines, and equipment. The other hull, outside the main hull, can be filled with either air or water. Water in the hull makes the submarine dense enough to sink. When the water is replaced by air, which is stored compressed in tanks, the submarine rises to the surface.

4 Put your container under the end of the tube to catch any overflowing water. Pour water into the bottle until it reaches the bottom of the tube but does not flow out through the tube.

5 Place the piece of modeling clay into the bottle of water. Water will flow through the tube and out into the container.

6 Weigh the container with the water in it. Because you set the scale to zero earlier with the container on top, it should now show the weight of just the water. Repeat the experiment with different objects—use some that float and some that sink.

FOLLOW-UP Diver density

Try another experiment to see how you can make an object float or sink by changing its density. You will need:

- *plastic ballpoint pen lid*
- *modeling clay*
- *water*
- *glass*
- *one-liter water bottle*

1 First, you need to make a pen-lid diver. Most pen lids have a small hole at the tip—plug it with a tiny blob of modeling clay.

Now put a larger blob of clay around the end of the lid's clip. Use just enough clay for the pen lid to stay afloat. Test this by putting the lid in a glass of water. Add clay to the lid until it sinks. At that point take off a very small amount of modeling clay. The diver should just float.

The pen lid has a small bubble of air trapped inside its tip, so it is less dense than water. Adding modeling clay, which is more dense than water, increases the density of the diver.

2 Fill the plastic bottle almost to the top with water, then put the pen-lid diver in the bottle, and screw on the bottle top.

3 Grip the bottle with both hands, and squeeze it firmly. What happens to the diver? The pen-lid diver should sink when the bottle is squeezed.

4 Releasing the bottle makes the pen-lid diver rise back to the surface. If this does not happen, try adding a little extra modeling clay to the end of the pen lid.

Small blob of clay to plug hole

Blob of clay large enough so that the pen lid just floats

ANALYSIS
Floating

Look closely at your results from the main activity. What do you notice about the weight of the objects compared to the weight of the overflow? You may find that the two measurements are roughly equal. You can use your results to plot a graph, like the one below, with the weight of the object along one axis and the weight of the overflow on the other axis. When you link up the points, they should make a roughly straight, diagonal line. The weight of the displaced water should be equal to the weight of the object in every case.

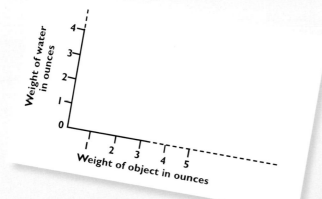

When an object floats, only part of the object is submerged. Only the underwater part of the object pushes aside, or displaces, water. However, the amount of water displaced is still equal to the weight of the whole object. A ship that is launched sinks into the ocean until the weight of the water it displaces is just equal to its own weight.

PEN-LID DIVER

Why does the diver sink when you squeeze the bottle? When you squash the bottle, you are squashing the water inside it. The water, in turn, squashes the air inside the pen lid. This makes the air more dense. This change in density makes the diver sink.

Many fish change their density in a similar way. Inside the fish is sac of air called a swim bladder. When the fish wants to go farther down, it squeezes the air in the bladder, making itself more dense. When the fish stops squeezing, it becomes less dense and rises.

Floating water

As water gets colder, it becomes denser. If you are swimming in the sea or a lake, you might feel the colder water deeper down. It stays deeper because it is more dense. Currents of warm water float on top of this denser, colder water. These warm currents cause changes in the air temperature and pressure above them. Warm water sea life uses these currents to migrate between areas of colder water. In some cases currents of warm water can cause changes on land, too. For example, although England is far north, temperatures there are warmed by light winds that blow in off seas warmed by the warm Gulf Stream.

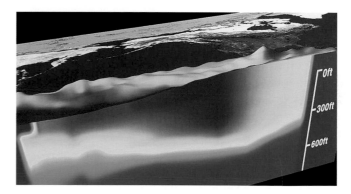

Warm ocean currents float on denser, cold waters, as this cross-section of the Pacific Ocean shows.

GLOSSARY

acceleration: The rate at which velocity changes.

amplitude: The size of a vibration. The amplitude of a pendulum's swing, for example, is how far it moves from its resting point.

angular momentum: Measure of the tendency of an object to keep on rotating; angular momentum equals the object's moment of inertia multiplied by its angular velocity.

angular velocity: The rate at which an object rotates.

compression: Squashing of an object or substance.

deceleration: The rate at which something changes its velocity as it slows down.

density: The mass of a substance per unit of volume.

drag: The slowing effect of friction on objects moving through a gas or liquid.

efficiency: The ratio of the amount of useful energy put out by a machine to the amount of energy put into it.

effort: The force that acts on a machine to move the load.

energy: Ability to do work. There are many different types of energy, including kinetic energy and potential energy, as well as heat, nuclear, chemical, and electrical energy.

force: Something that tends to change the velocity of an object—that is, changes its speed or direction.

frequency: The number of times per second that a process repeats itself.

friction: The force between two solid objects that are rubbing together, tending to slow them.

fulcrum: The point around which a lever turns.

gravity: An attractive force between two or more objects. Gravity is hardly noticeable for small objects, but big ones, such as moons, planets, and stars, strongly attract nearby objects.

gyroscope: A disk mounted so that it can spin freely in all directions.

inertia: Resistance of an object to changes in velocity. The greater an objects' mass, the greater its inertia.

kinetic energy: The energy that any object has due to its movement. Kinetic energy can be converted into other forms of energy as the object is brought to rest. For example, falling water can generate electricity.

lever: A bar that turns on a fulcrum to move a load.

load: The force that a machine acts against.

machine: A device that changes the strength or direction of the force used to perform a task.

mass: A measure of how much matter there is in an object. The greater the mass, the more the object resists changes in its velocity, and the more strongly it attracts other objects by gravity and is attracted by them.

mechanical advantage: The ratio of the load moved by a machine to the effort.

moment of inertia: A measure of how easy it is to change the rate of rotation of an object. It depends on the mass and shape of the object.

momentum: The tendency of an object to keep moving.

It equals the object's mass multiplied by its velocity.

orbit: The path followed by an object such as a planet or a spacecraft, around another object when it is acted on by gravity alone.

pendulum: An object that is hung from a fixed point and is free to swing.

period: The time it takes for a cyclic process to repeat itself—for example, the time for a pendulum to make one swing.

perpetual motion machine: A machine that could keep doing useful work forever with no energy being put in. Such a machine is impossible.

potential energy: The energy that an object has because of its position. For example, a person standing on a chair has gravitational potential energy because he or she could jump off, turning the potential energy into kinetic energy.

precession: The slow, circling motion of a fast-spinning gyroscope or top.

pressure: Force of compression per unit of area.

pulley: A simple pulley is a suspended wheel over which a rope passes. A person can lift a weight attached to one end of the rope by pulling down on the other end. A compound pulley is an arrangement of a rope and several wheels that gives a mechanical advantage greater than 1, so that a load greater than the effort can be lifted.

quantum theory: The scientific theory describing the existence and behavior of subatomic particles.

relativity: A theory developed by the German-born U.S. physicist Albert Einstein in the early 20th century. Einstein showed that distances and times are different for different observers, depending on how fast they are moving. Furthermore, the speed of light in empty space is the same for all observers, and nothing can travel faster than it. Einstein explained gravity as a distortion of space and time.

resonance: A vibration that is triggered by another vibration. For example, if a note is played on an instrument held near a piano, the piano strings will start to sound, or resonate.

speed: The rate of change of distance with time of a body moving in a straight line or a continuous curve.

stability: The tendency for an object to stay in one position or to keep moving in the same direction. A book lying on its side is stable in position. The planets' motions around the Sun are also relatively stable, since they do not change over a very long time, as long as there is no outside disturbance.

stress: Amount of force applied to some object per unit of area (for instance, the force stretching a wire divided by the wire's cross-sectional area).

tension: A force that tends to stretch an object.

torque: A turning force on an object caused by equal and opposite forces that do not act along the same line.

upthrust: The upward force on an object in a liquid or a gas. If it is greater than the weight of the object, the object floats.

velocity: The speed of an object together with the direction of the object's movement.

weight: The downward force on an object due to gravity.

work: The energy expended when a force moves an object in the direction of the force.

SET INDEX